25 Ways to Overcome a Bad Reputation in the News Media

A media crisis personal guidebook
by

Dennis E. Adonis

Published by

Inspired
inPrint

25 Ways to Overcome a Bad Reputation ....

Written by: Dennis E. Adonis

Copyright © May 2017

Cover photos model: Dennis E. Adonis

Cover photos inspired by: Luis Molinero

Connect with the Publisher: **info@inspiredinprint.com**

Connect with the author at: **adonisbooks@gmail.com**

"People would say bad things about you; because it is the only way their insignificant self can feel better than you"

– Dennis E. Adonis

Acknowledgements

I will forever remain thankful to the Creator for the strength and inspiration that he has given unto me to write this book, so that I can truly be a motivator and an inspiration to others in their time of media torment and pain.

As always, I am acknowledging my wife Sedella for being supportive of my struggles against the wrongs that were showered upon me, and all of the things that were misreported about me.

In the same way, I wish to honour my children for their strength and enduring support in my quest for ultimate redemption.

Without a doubt I am also thankful to my friend and staff Ms. Anesicia McPherson for standing by my side during some of my most challenging and darkest hours.

But even so, I could not had won the battle against media degradation without the continued support of my friends; notably, Mr. Christopher "Aristo Cat" Humphrey, my assistant Ms. Malika Callender, Ms. Oneka Daniels, Ms. Bibi Inshan, Mr. Michael of Sharon's Building – Guyana, Mr. James Seaforth, Bentley English, Mark Walcott, my brother Carl Adonis, Mr. Lynton Luke, "Lemonade" Bunbury, Simba Doris, Marlon Cruickshank, Mr. Michael Lutchman, my parents, all of my siblings, my uncles, aunts, and cousins, among others.

Inspired
inPrint

Other related inspiring books by the author

■

25 Ways to overcome separation & loneliness

■

25 Ways to overcome depression and stress

■

25 Ways to find your ideal soul-mate

■

25 Ways to find sustained happiness

■

25 ways to be a better parent

■

www.inspiredinprint.com

Table of Contents

● Introduction

■ The role of the media & your reputation

There is an old adage which reason that *"the pen is mightier than the sword"*.

In other words, something that is written and published has the capacity to do more harm to a person, a business entity, or an entire nation, than the sharp edges of a thousand swords.

But even though this adage is there as an established sense of fact, it is often kept out of our focus, as our minds seem to be more preemptively fearful of those things that are physical or tangible, rather than having any prophylactic concern for a bundle of words printed on a piece of newspaper, or a news presenter babbling away on our television screen.

For most of us, or rather our subconscious, those words on a paper or of a babbling presenter is not our life's priorities (or so we thought).

By nature, we somehow tend to keep the relevance of the news media in our lives to an almost subliminal minimum.

As a matter of fact, we often underestimate the almost immeasurable power of the news media, and its profound capacity to influence people's minds or their views, and even our own personal lives.

Because in reality, the world relies on the economic predictions of the news media, and the opinions of journalists and news media outlets in order to make informed decisions.

From an update on the weather, to the prevailing currency market, and updates on the latest global news events, our life and our ability to decide, now heavily rely on the news media more than we had actually thought.

For example, the sale of this book can be increased by a thousand percent if the New York Times add it to their best seller list, or if it is featured on the Oprah channel as a must read.

And even if it doesn't make any sense to the average reader, the public would still be inclined to buy it because the New York Times or the Oprah Channel say that they should do so.

Similarly, if Time Magazine names you as one of the most influential persons of the 21st century, or one of the best economists that ever lived, that is what the world would accept and approve of, even if you don't have a clue about economics.

In the same way, if those same media outlets tell the world that you are a crooked or horrible person, the world would believe that, whether there is enough facts to substantiate that characterization or not.

That being said, and if you can understand or appreciate my point, you would agree that the world is indirectly reliant on the news media as a primary source of information and a source of reference more than any other medium on the planet.

Therefore, depending on what is out there about you in the media, that is what people tend to use to evaluate and determine your reputation, among other things.

And because of that, you would further agree that the news media can either make or break any person or anything, by publishing either positive or negative content about them in print or online.

By extension, the news media practically holds the "Sword of Damocles" over your reputation, and in essence, can decide whether you live your life with a good one or whether you struggle through the perils of time with a bad one.

And while it will be great to be on the good side of the news media so as to preserve your good reputation, that is usually not a choice for you to make.

But whenever the media spills the bad reputation oil on you, then in that case, you have a choice.

And that choice is to either stay with that dirty reputation oil spilled out all over your skin, or be brave enough to follow my lead in this book, and let me show you how you can survive those dirty reputation oil spills, and how to clean yourself up too.

After all, my reputation was similarly thrown in the dirty oil gutter (and maybe is still being thrown in the gutter) by one group of people with one clear agenda.

But if I was able to survive it, and was still able to achieve my life goals without any hindrances; - so can you.

● The importance of your reputation

One of the most prized possessions that any company, any place, any country, or a person can have is their good reputation.

After all, it is the one piece of celestial asset that walks before us, walks with us, and walks after us, all at the same time.

It is more or less of a virtual character identification card or a unique ubiquitous fingerprint by which we are known or by which other people measures us in order to make considerations in their dealings with us.

Throughout the passage of time, it has been used as the most credible source of reference for a man's character, and has also functioned as the most effective form of measurement in the generic weighting of trust among people.

And though it is not an element that you can physically grab, feel, touch or taste; it is a rather virtual part of your very existence, of which you have no other choice than to carry; and to work hard to protect, throughout your lifetime.

Because life lessons has repeatedly taught us that, without a good reputation, your life, your career, your personal development, dreams and aspirations, your marriage, your pride, your dignity, and your seal of trust can be swiftly thrown out of the window, often without a chance of ever regaining it, once it is lost.

After all, we subconsciously rely on our reputation to build new business relationships, to obtain credit, to secure a job, to build trust, to be secure, to survive, to build the morale of our children, to feel appreciated, and to be a positive inspiration to all of the people around us.

And though some of these very things can be achieved with or without a good reputation, a number of psychological and depressing issues can arise, if you have to be repeatedly forcing people to trust you or to see the good in you (for example).

Because in reality; most companies would not be too happy to do business with a man who was once featured in the media as a pyramid schemer, a finance pilfering agent, or a fraudster (just to name a few).

Likewise no community or average thinking person would feel safe to welcome a new resident who was once featured in the news as a terrorist, a child molester or a stalker.

After all, their natural human instinct would force them to consider their self-interest against yours, and their family's safety against any benefit of having you around.

For most of them, any meaningful engagement with you, even indirectly, would not be to their benefit or their interest, unless your character can specifically resonate with some sort of service or any benefitting skillset that they may need.

What is interesting today is that people do not need your permission or need you to show them a specific document to make their own determination when it comes to your reputation.

With mankind's reliance on technology and specifically the internet to make initial reference checks on practically anything; - it is almost impossible for you to escape a potential internet search of your person.

And whenever something negative or character-degrading pops up about you, a person's mind would be naturally inclined to promptly go into defense mode, or to immediately react to any dealings with you with profound caution.

Because even if your true character does not resonate with none of the presumably negative things that are established in an online search feed, people and companies still tend to initially rely on it as a possibly reliable third-party reference note or a potentially trusted piece of information that can serve as a virtual character reference for you.

And if those online feeds have effectively discredited you, especially in a negative or derogatory form, then you would certainly appreciate the value of a good reputation, and how effective this piece of unseen element can be to your very survival.

But then again, there have been many cases where some negative online results of a person's reputation did not necessarily impact their dealings with people and companies, mainly because those reputation negativities were mostly mild in nature.

As a matter of fact, reputation in itself is divided into twelve main categories, which entails;

(1) No reputation at all,

(2) A concealed reputation,

(3) A complex reputation,

(4) A concocted reputation

(5) A questionable reputation,

(6) An unstable reputation

(7) A checkered reputation

(8) A bad reputation

(9) An acceptable reputation,

(10) A fitting reputation,

(11) A good reputation,

(12) A revered reputation

But for the sake and context of this book, our discussions are intended to focus primarily on two of those categories, which entails a bad reputation and a good reputation; - of course, which is mostly because of their commonality in our daily lives, and the fact that the other categories are often classed interchangeably with either a good or a bad reputation, in any case.

However, as a matter of essential knowledge or to avert any confusion, it will be necessary that I discuss these various categories of the reputation scale with you, momentarily.

● What really is your reputation?

The definition for the word reputation can be quite elusive depending on the context in which you are examining it.

However, it generally resonates with the thoughts, inclinations, and beliefs or widespread belief about the characteristics and behavioral profile of someone or something.

Language researchers have long established that "reputation" which came from the Latin word *reputationem*, and which is to mean "consideration", would have had to do with the consideration that one person has to make for the other, as it relates to the element of trust.

But for the sake of not wanting to create any confusion or to dispute the definition of others, I was able to better determine that; - Reputation is the method by which the mind or a person measures the trust levels, reliability, and worthiness of another human being, a product, a service, or anything that can be both tangible or intangible, existing, and even non-existent.

While reputation is generally measured mostly between the range of good and bad, it also has other subconscious measurement levels or categories which usually determine the manner and way in which society or a community interacts with each person.

● Different categories of reputation

Now, as I had mentioned earlier, reputation in itself is primarily divided into twelve main categories, which of course can be transcended into eighteen other sub-categories.

But since only the basic aspects of this subject is what really matters as it relates to our discussions in this book, I will only provide a brief understanding of the twelve main categories for reference.

1 – No reputation at all; -

While this phrase might be more synonymous with a spiritual reference that was made in the bible at Philippians 2:7, and within a biblical context, there is no other actual record of its meaning, or correct use, except in urban communication culture.

Because in reality; there is no agreement that a person "having no reputation at all" can actually exist within the context of humanity's behavioral measurements.

Hence, the term is generally used interchangeably for someone so unknown, undocumented, unseen, or sometimes irrelevant that the no reputation (good or bad) of the person can be conceived or be attested to.

Science has also indirectly assigned persons of unsound mind, the criminally insane, those having split personality issues, those of a certain level of spectrum disorders, or those with serious mental challenges within this category, since their true reputation cannot be actually measured.

This may so, because it is as if the moral identity and real character of the person does not exist on a fair scale that is enough for a genuine assessment to be made.

And in such instances, people or an entity would generally prefer to accommodate a person whose reputation is known (whether good or bad), than to interface with a person with no reputation at all.

2 – A concealed reputation; -

This is a person who either deliberately makes it difficult for his reputation to be assessed or whose lifestyle is so clandestine that it is actually difficult to say whether they have a good or a bad reputation.

These types of persons can be very social or non-social, or can be an open book that you still can't read.

Their methods of concealment are generally natural, but they can also go to great lengths just to make it difficult for you to actually get a true assessment of their reputation.

While a person with a concealed reputation may be able to get around somewhat, they often do not stick to one group of friends, one place or one job for a long time, since they are either afraid of exposure, or of being misinterpreted in their character.

3 - Complex reputation;

- A complex reputation holder is someone who can have a bad reputation at one place and very good one at another.

For example, a person can be considered a pick-pocket thief in the city streets of Rome targeting unsuspecting tourists, but is known as committed, hardworking, honest and dedicated father back at home in Madrid.

Similarly a person can be a great and honest nanny to her employers in London, but a notorious shoplifter in her home country across the Pacific.

The simple issue here with this sort of reputation is that the person may not be trusted much in one place, but can be trusted and vouched for in another.

It is more common among people in migrant populations, who may not have an issue with the idea of compromising their character in one place, in order to find comfort in another.

4 - A concocted reputation; -

A person with a concocted reputation may best fit with someone whose behavioral tendencies or overall demeanor does not commensurate with who they say they are, who people may have said they are, or you was cause to believe they are.

For example, a person, their resume or their representative can effectively say that they are an expert in mathematics, but is having a difficulty giving you the answer for 2+2.

In another instance, a person claiming to be an original singer of a Grammy awarded song, should not be afraid of singing the song on stage.

The reality here is that the person might not have a criminal history, a different identity, or a bad reputation per say, but is more or less living a concocted or pretended life which can practically cause more harm than good for themselves and the people around them.

Persons of this nature are generally incapable of holding a good job, a marriage or friendships for long periods.

This is often because of their fear of their character being realized or because they were found out to be the complete opposite of who they say they are, or whom people were caused to believe them to be.

5 – Questionable reputation; -

A person with this type of reputation is often controversial in their actions and sayings, but often see no wrong in their conduct. It can also be attributed to someone with a dubious or a shady reputation.

While they may not necessarily be a Homer Simpson or a Peter Griffin in their respective popular television series, the handling of situations often place someone with this type of reputation on a precipice between good and bad.

A fine example can be a well-respected preacher promoting sex-before-marriage, or a popular and loved actor supporting all forms of segregation between two races.

So while people may appreciate a person's work or their doings, they are often divided or forced to discredit them in as much that they are no longer sure about the sincerity of the person's reputation.

This can also apply to any professional person (for example a prominent attorney or an accountant) whose representation of a client's responsibilities has tantamount to them committing an act of fraud against their client, and the issue is thrown into the public domain.

Again, while other people may appreciate the quality of their work, an existing character issue (as mentioned earlier) would have reduced the public's trust in their office, and thus bring their reputation into question.

6 - Unstable reputation; -

If you know of a very good doctor whose work is unquestionable, but who sometimes gets involved in bar fights and pub brawls or would not think twice to publicly ventilate his spats about his wife, then you can certainly have an idea where I am coming from.

People with this sort of reputation are not necessarily bad people. But they might be suffering from underlying issues which would often transform them into another state whenever they are upset, provoked, stimulated, or intoxicated.

They are usually very apologetic in their normal state, and are good at explaining or justifying a flaw in their conduct or persona when confronted.

However, a person with this type of reputation can face employment problems, or be restraint from being promoted to a responsible position, because of their unstable reputation.

7 - Checkered reputation; -

A person with a checkered reputation, would be someone whose good reputation has been intermingled with bad episodes or reputation damaging episodes earlier in his life.

It generally fits with people who would have either been publicly brought to account for a well-reported act of dishonesty, a financial or moral discrepancy, or who was arrested, imprisoned, or otherwise caused to be brought before a court to answer to a criminal charge.

While some people may have been quietly brought to account for improprieties in the past, and outside of the public's hearing; they can still be clandestinely placed into this reputation category; - and can still face employment and business opportunity hurdles within a particular career network.

8 - Bad reputation; -

Well if the word "bad" itself cannot get the message home to you then maybe you really don't get it.

Because by all accounts, a person with a bad reputation is generally someone that people does not trust, or whose integrity has been classified as criminally inclined, morally uneven, lowly in conduct or simply dishonorable because of their general character, or something they must had done, or suspected to have done.

A person with a bad reputation in itself may not necessarily has to be a bad person by nature, since their character or conduct (or alleged conduct) is what they are generally evaluated by.

On the other hand, a person who has a bad reputation in the views of one group of people may not necessarily be considered as bad by another.

This is usually common in political circles, business groupings, or in cases of disputes turn violent, or actions turning immoral; - for which one group may see no wrong in their actions; but which can be found to be atrocious by the other.

Furthermore, the extent to which people are accused of having a bad reputation would often stretch way beyond a man being characterized for an alleged crime or misconduct by the media.

In other words, it can very well be considered bad among one group, one community, or one network of people, who may have or believe that they have justifiable reasons to consider another person's reputation as "bad".

And in despite of the fact that some characters can indeed be easily identified as bad, most reputation monitors have agreed that there are no fixed rules or proper limitation in latitude when considering someone as an individual with a bad reputation.

Hence, the depth and overall scope that is used to categorize a person as having a bad reputation can either be factual, deliberately selective, generalized, flawed, circumstantial, or even periodic in some instances.

But regardless of how you may view it, a bad reputation can be easily attributed to anyone who does not fit with the good character description of any group of people, a society or even a country itself.

9 - An acceptable reputation; -

This type of reputation is more individualized than broad-based, since it is usually only considered applicable to a person based upon the average consideration granted by a group of people, an organization, a movement, a cause, a community, a city, or a country as a whole.

A person with an acceptable reputation can be someone who either had a bad reputation, a checkered reputation, an unstable reputation, a complex reputation, or a questionable reputation, but has showed signs of reform, is willing to reform, have been somewhat reformed, or can be reformed.

In those circumstances, an employer, a country, an organization, or any relevant body of people can find it more benefitting to accept you as you are for a greater good, or to consider your inclusion for some other reason that does not threaten or risk the interest of the considering party or that party's interest.

A typical example may be a man who was wanted by a country for an international crime, but whose witness statements or information can contribute to a greater good of that country.

This can also be attributed to people with certain careers, professions, and skillsets that are needed by an organization or a country, who may be willing to employ or accommodate you for the benefit of the country or the organization's success, regardless of your reputation or other attributes that would have ordinarily been an issue.

10 - A fitting reputation; -

Someone is usually granted a fitting reputation because it is a necessity in order to either grant you, award you, or credit you for something that is of importance to a person, a company, or a country.

For example if you are wanted for banking fraud in a country, but has saved a thousand lives after stopping a terrorist from detonating a bomb (for example); that country might be willing to downplay your previously bad, checkered, or questionable reputation, so that you may be fitting enough to receive the appropriate commendation, award or reward for your heroism.

While this is rare, a number of people were able to restart their lives with a fitting reputation that was granted to them by other countries or their native country.

11 - A good reputation ; -

Well I know this may be envious to the average mind, but like everything else, there are a lot of people with a reputation that is good enough to earn our general or national trust, as it relates to almost anything.

And these are the people who often have a greater shot at the most pluses in life, and who are most likely to get a free-pass for most of the reputation-reliant things that are usually difficult for the average person to obtain.

By comparison, they can acquire these things with some degree of ease; and which can range from a simple bank loan, to a resettlement visa for another country.

Therefore, we can all agree that a good reputation is actually a great thing to have, and an important element in our quest for survival and success.

But of course, it is not an easy factor in our life to protect. However, as indirectly explained earlier, a good reputation can go a long way, and can provide us with an immediate reference tool for many of the comforts and aspirations that we may need in life.

12 - A revered reputation; -

A revered reputation is a somewhat elusive quest for most of us, but which goes beyond just a good reputation.

To better make my point, people who are revered such as a prophet or other known people such as the Queen, Mother Teresa, the Dalai Lama, and the Pope, are often so revered and supported that their good reputation are almost near impossible for anyone to destroy or for any news media outfit to impact negatively enough.

As a matter of fact, merely criticizing someone who has attained the revered reputation status can usually have serious repercussions for the criticizing party or even those that condone the criticism.

Attaining this higher category on the reputation scale is generally difficult. As a matter of fact, it can take years, a remarkable occurrence, or a multitude of factors in order for it to be achieved.

In other words, it has to be strenuously and appropriately earned, and not handed over to you in a package or on a platter.

And by most accounts, it will take more than just creating a few good miracles to achieve the revered reputation status.

Though there are people who are quite iconic, such as film stars and political figures; their adulation by one group or an international group should not be mistakenly placed into this category of the reputation scale.

● How you can lose your reputation

Losing your reputation is much easier and realistic than you may actually think. And can range from the simplest to the broadest of reasons.

But in any case, the news media basically holds the monopoly on deciding whether a man keeps his reputation or not.

And while the media can target your wonderful name in various ways, they can certainly make you kiss your good reputation goodbye in either of the following circumstances.

■ 1 - You commit a crime or were accused of committing a crime

Of all ways in which you can lose your good reputation, none can be more impacting than the news media negatively associating your name with a criminal allegation or a crime in itself.

And associating your name in itself does not necessarily mean that you are the person who had actually committed a crime or is believed to have committed the crime.

All that is needed is for the news media to tie you to the crime, or by associating you with the alleged perpetrator, or by demonstrating that you presumably had knowledge, had uphold, or entertain a person in the commissioning of a crime.

Alternatively, if a company that you manage or holds some sort of major directorship role in, has been found to be criminally culpable for something of public interest, that would be all a journalist might need to criminally destroy your name.

And depending on your social status or rather who you are on the social ladder, crime can have a lasting or even a permanently negative effect on your reputation.

Moreover, the nature of the crime and its scope, or the allegations itself can practically force you to say adios amigos to your good name.

The problem with criminal allegations is that even if you are exonerated or you are proven to be innocent, all of the primary negative exposures that you may have already had in the media would forever stand at the forefront of your reputation gauge.

After all, the human mind has a terrible way of separating an allegation from the fact of a matter, and moreover, an extreme difficulty in separating facts from fiction in the media.

Therefore, if your name was once aligned with a criminal allegation, then it might take another half of your lifetime to rebuild your reputation thereafter.

■ 2 - You made a misguided quote or a misguided statement

A lot of people have found their reputation being buried by the media simply because they had made a statement or said something that was misguided, misinterpreted or misinformed, and which was blown out of proportion by the news media.

This can range from a simple issue such as aggravating a non-influential rights group, to uttering words or statements that are either directly or indirectly racial in its tone, regardless of if it was done privately or publicly.

And there are too many examples of this scenario, which I am sure will be lengthy enough for a complete television season.

But just for a random case in point, we can take famous WWE star Hulk Hogan as a fine example.

A few years ago, when it was discovered that Hogan had made some racist remarks (though privately) as it relates to his daughter's relationship with an African American man, his sponsors and the WWE immediately degraded his reputation in as much that his name was scrubbed from the organization's website, and removed from the coveted WWE Hall of Fame.

And before he knew it, all of the good reputation milestones that the once distinguished wrestler and film star had earned throughout his lifetime were thrown into the gutter.

After all, the media was good at ensuring that no company or business professional will ever want to do business with Hogan again.

■ **3 - You were involved or were accused of being involved in morally unacceptable behavior**

While in many cases a wife might be reluctant to file a police report against an abusive husband, or a friend might be reluctant to report you for touching his wife inappropriately while on a drunken escapade; - you might not necessarily be in a safe zone if the news media highlight these moral discrepancies about your character.

Because, no company or professional person would want to associate their entity or person with a man that is considered a wife beater or an accused sexual predator.

So from the moment the media outfits you as an immoral character or has placed you in the immoral conduct category; be assured that your reputation would be flying out the window in haste.

It is not that your critics are perfect or may be any better in their life actions than you are.

It is mostly because you were caught, and your exposure would certainly mean some great readership benefits for the news media.

But of course, such a derogatory highlight in the

press can be an unforgiving grinding mill in the face of your good reputation.

■ 4 - You are accused of endorsing certain types of unpopular traits or organizations

If the news media links you to criminal organization, a hate group, a terrorist organization, a notorious criminal, a societal outcast, a war crime, money laundering, narco-trafficking, human trafficking, being a part of an oppressive political regime, or being involved in certain tribal sadistic practices such as female genital mutilation, then you can definitely wave your good reputation goodbye.

Because from the moment these sort of accusations appear in the press, most countries would not want to grant you a visa, neither would any established company or person want to engage in any form of business dealings with you.

After all, the mere media-fueled perception that you are affiliated with certain immoralities; or is sympathetic towards a certain cause; certain organizations, or traits; - are mostly already enshrined in many countries laws, beliefs, or cultures, which would have long pre-determined your reputation, in any case.

Therefore, if your reputation is twisted into any of these unpopular traits, then you will certainly have a hard time escaping any of them.

Moreover, your once good reputation would eventually find itself being buried in the proverbial dead reputation box, six feet under.

■ **5 - You have made a grievous blunder on social media**

Facebook, twitter, Instagram, WhatsApp, Skype and dozens of other similar social media tools have become an integral part of our life in so many ways, that most of us can't function, keep abreast of things, remember birthdays and anniversaries, communicate, or keep in touch with our loved ones without it.

As a matter of fact, most people today would only express their emotions, their opinions, and their voices on social media.

Psychologist have long concluded that a person's social media presence, posts, and other elements can tell you a number of things about that person's daily life, their challenges, their views, their fears, and more.

So if the law enforcement agencies can use your social media profiles to gather information about you, what would make you think that the news media is not doing the same?

Because like everything else, social media platforms have their flip side.

After all, people from all walks of life are often forced to send out a Tweet or a Facebook post whenever they want to vent their frustration at something or whenever they are seeking the support or response from their social-media friends regarding a frustrating subject matter.

However, most will usually rely on the posting of photos and statements to solicit Likes and favourable comments which is a psychological tonic to build their self-esteem, especially about their appearance or their opinions.

And all it usually takes for the media to ruin your reputation, is a simple mistaken post, or a post that seems to criticize or support something that is contentious.

Alternatively, a controversial photo of yourself, your family or any similar situation on social media can also serve its purpose much to the advantage of the news media, who would certainly have no difficulty utilizing your blunder to ruin your reputation.

So if you are into social postings, and the realms of social networking, then you must be very careful about what you post in the public domain.

Because, it might very well come back one day, to haunt your good reputation.

■ 6 - Your lies have catch up with you

Lying about something that is of public interest, and then being exposed by the news media as a liar later, can certainly see your reputation being thrown out of the ring.

This is generally more impacting and devastating when you are in an office of public trust or hold a position where the public or consumers are greatly relying on your trust and honesty.

And if the people who had trusted you before found out via the news media that you have lied to them, especially on a great scale, then you can be sure that your reputation score in their book will certainly wind down to zero.

■ 7 - Someone paid a media house or a journalist to smear your reputation

Hired journalism is probably one of the oldest tricks in the book of compulsory reputation degradation.

And one of the oldest victims of this trick would have been the late civil rights advocate, political leader, avid writer, publisher, journalist, businessman, and orator, Marcus Mosiah Garvey who was repeatedly featured as a fraudster in multiple publications across the United States between 1919 to 1923, mostly as a covert request of the BOI, which is now the FBI (Federal Bureau of Investigations).

While his reputation was destroyed for the sake of having him deported from the United States to Jamaica, the news media never corrected their wrongs about Garvey until the early 20th century when it was accepted that the repeated classification of Garvey as a fraudster was falsely attached to his reputation only for one reason.

And while we do not want to drown ourselves out in history, Garvey's experiences on how easily one's reputation can be destroyed, remains relevant to modern lessons.

Because even today, and even more widespread than in the days of Marcus Garvey, the lifting or sinking of someone's reputation can be easily achieved, since it now carries a generic price tag.

After all, public perception of a person or their product can often determine that person's successes or failures on many fronts.

Because if (for example) a major news media outlet has labelled you as a match-fixing and crooked referee, then there is no way the public would trust your judgment on a game, and there is no way a sporting organization would want to hire you to put their gaming event's reputation in jeopardy.

And one of the easiest ways to destroy a person's reputation, is by hiring a journalist or by patronizing a media house financially to do it.

Therefore, you can easily find your reputation being wrecked by a hired news outlet or a broad section of media houses via the said sponsored attack of your character.

While this practice is quite common in dirty politics, it is even more widespread in the world of business.

For example if you are selling a product or service that would seriously rival your competitor's own, that affected entity can utilize hired journalism to attack your character and ruin your reputation; all with the intention of running you out of business.

And from my very own experiences, it is one of the most painful ways to see your reputation go.

In other words, I can safely attest to this because I had personally gone through numerous episodes of media blackmailing and reputation-degrading; in as much that I can tell you that this is an almost unavoidable way in which you can see your reputation being derailed.

Especially if it is persistent; and is bent mostly on negatively characterizing you.

■ **8 - Your name is being targeted by the news media for profiteering.**

If a person is of high social media and readership value, is popular, is controversial, is looked up to, or is a reader demanding figure, news media would often make these sorts of persons a target for repeated news listing.

Because the more negative and controversial stories one can carry about the Queen, a head of state or some famous figure, the more readership that publication would be able to pull to its base.

But while news media networks may be targeting someone for repeated news items on their perceived controversies or issues, that person's reputation is practically being destroyed in each instance.

And before you know it, the affected can eventually develop a terrible media reputation, when in reality that is not who they really are.

■ 9 - You have offended someone and they want to get back at you

Well, for some people who can't seem to find a way to physically harm you, getting back at you or punishing you via embarrassing media exposures, always seem to be the preferred option.

This can either take the form of using third parties to set you up, file a trumped-up police complaint against you, or directly label certain degrading accusations against you or your business entity.

And since this is one of the oldest tricks in the book, many persons are often targeted this way, and would often never realize that someone was trying to get back at them by ruining their reputation via the news media.

■ 10 - You were erroneously named in a nasty article

Sometimes, though rarely, the ruining of your reputation in the media could have been a genuine mistake either on the part of the author or editor of the reputation ruining article.

And unless that offending article is actually deleted or modified on the respective news media website, and a retraction is broadly published in the print edition of the offending publication, then rest assure that your good reputation will be chipping away slowly, but surely.

For most of the part, your detractors do not look for retractions; neither would the retraction gain the same level of exposure as the damaging article itself, both online and in print.

■ 11 - Your children, spouse, or a close relative have blundered or is accused of a crime

While you can try as hard as you can to ensure that you do not contribute to the tarnishing of your good reputation, your children, your spouse or a close relative can still cause your reputation to be thrown into the gutter.

As a matter of fact, there have been many cases where husbands were forced to resign from a position because of something criminal or morally degrading that their offspring or their wife had done (vice versa), and which is often misinterpreted as the general moral or criminal character of the entire family.

In essence, it is thought that a husband who cannot control or accept responsibility for the actions of his wife is not responsible enough to be trusted by others.

The same lesson can apply to a parent who might be heading an anti-drug trafficking organization (for example), and their own son was arrested for drug smuggling or some other related criminal activity.

Such an incident would certainly place that parent in a tough position, and would obviously give the impression that he was either covering up for his son, or his son was indirectly benefitting from his father's job position.

As a result, public trust and respect for that person's office would be lost and their reputation itself would certainly grind to a new low.

And in such a case, the media can very well use the incident or any other blunders of one spouse or a child to derail the good reputation of the other.

■ 12 - Someone who was (or is) close to you unveils a dirty secret or something negative about you

Like every other person on the social ladder of life, every prominent or relevant person also has someone that they trust with many of their life secrets or who was able to observe the most confidential aspects of their lives.

From a trusted personal assistant, to a secretary, a butler, a personal driver, or some other confidante, you might be surprised at the number of people who may actually have a hold on many of your little dirty secrets.

And not just any secret; but the ones that can actually send you to jail, destroy your marriage or put your reputation on the line.

But even though most of these people might go to their graves with information about you that could have actually destroyed your good reputation, there are others who may be more than willing to trade it for money.

And when a trusted source decides to sell inside information about you, the most interested buyer of your dirty little secrets, damaging photos, or questionable doings are always the news media.

Therefore, if the people that are close to you have an issue with you, wants to profit from you, blackmail you, or simply wants to destroy you, then they may very well be in a good position to do so by either directly or clandestinely revealing degrading information about you.

And when the public gets negative information about you from someone that is close or was close to you, you can bet that most of them will be more than happy to believe it.

In such a case, you can very well kiss your good reputation goodbye.

● Rebuilding your reputation

Rebuilding a media tarnished reputation, especially when it is spread across multiple publications is an extremely difficult task by any angle, but not outright impossible.

In reality, the loss of one's reputation is usually measured within a scale of one to ten, since this will certainly identify the severity of a person's trust challenge or reputation itself.

However, while the average reputation issues that does not make it to the media can put you at a loss of somewhere between one and five if confined to a particular group of people; - that number usually starts from a massive five on the reputation scale from the moment it is reported negatively in the media.

That in itself can provide you with an idea of how dangerous negative media reporting can be for a person's good reputation.

Even though, it would usually either make a slight drop by one bar, or a slight rise by the same ratio a few weeks later on the reputation scale, any form of negative media reporting will still be a challenge to repair regardless of the time that had elapsed.

In essence, any form of reputation damage that was instigated by the news media is often extensive, and can be very much difficult to rebuild.

This is often the case, because people's beliefs are usually always prejudiced to what was already fed to their minds, and which in turn can promote their natural reluctance to give up on what they would have already believed.

And even from my own experiences, rebuilding a media tarnished reputation can take a variety of forms.

This is usually because each situation would often require that you utilize a unique or individualized method, depending on various circumstances such as the scope of the incident and the general character of the person whose reputation was targeted.

Therefore, what may work for your dealings with Peter, would not necessarily work for Paul, and so on.

Nonetheless, most media tarnished reputation rebuilding processes work with an inter-related set of rules; but does not require the same group of considerations; since this is practically reliant on how unique each individual situation may be.

In other words, even though the rules are almost the same, there is not necessarily a generic method of approach to reputation rebuilding.

However, there are some methods that can be considered acceptable in their scope, but not necessarily a one size fits all method either.

But based upon my own research and experiences, there are at least twenty five broad-based instructions that you can follow as a general reputation rebuilding and character repair tool, if you are to seriously recreate the element of trust and respect for your person again.

These twenty five steps are divided into three interrelated phases, which are (1) discovery and response, (2) surviving the ordeal, and (3) restoration and redemption; as we will discuss hereafter.

25 steps to overcome a bad reputation in the media

1 - Accept that in life, things will go wrong

In despite of our desire to escape all of the perils and disappointments in life, there is still one rule of faith that we must be willing to accept if we are to actually conquer the challenges of life.

And that rule is that no matter how hard you may try, *things can go wrong, and things will go wrong*.

Historically, there have been too many repeated but evidently failed attempts by mankind to either eradicate the issues that have made our lives miserable, or try to pacify individual issues, in a bid to perfect one's life so that no ill or wrongs can befall oneself.

By extension, we have all tried to live an almost perfect life, or one that is basically free from all of the troubled elements of the world; especially those individualized situations such as a troubled relationship or a financial matter that can make our lives miserable even when it does not has anything to do with us, directly.

Hence, a utopia of life or a perfected life, though practically impossible, has been a long-lasting quest by mankind to escape the realities of a sometimes complex world.

But then again, no matter how hard you may try, there is never such a thing as a perfected life, or a full life that is free from the usual challenges which can range from a simple health concern, to a disappointing business deal or an intricate marital issue.

Because no matter how hard we try to perfect ourselves, our situation, or our paths in life, things will go wrong, and have always gone wrong.

And once you can first understand and accept that things can go wrong, then your mind can be better conditioned to deal with the varied element of wrongs, and their direct impact upon your reputation or upon the reputation of the people that are closest to you.

2 - Wake up to reality when things go wrong

Now, we can all tolerate the imaginary scenario of a robber lay waiting and pointing a gun to our head in his quest to retrieve whatever little valuables we may have.

In such a brief imaginary scenario, our hearts would not be racing or sweats would not be running down our faces, because it is nothing more than a thought that had crossed our mind while we sit in the comfort of our home.

Because in reality, imagining something and actually coming face to face with such a drama, would definitely be two completely different scenarios.

For if we were actually placed in such a real situation our hearts will be racing, our lives might flash before our eyes, and we might be shivering in cold sweat even after the ordeal is over.

To make my point, there is a big difference between the fantasy and reality of something.

In the same way, when something goes wrong, our first line of defense is usually to plunge into a state of psychological disbelief that a wrong against our person or character has actually occurred.

But one of the worst forms of psychological weaknesses that can overpower any person, is their failure to understand and accept the reality that something has gone wrong.

Simply put, you must first be mentally prepared to accept reality when something actually goes wrong.

So if you wake one morning and see a horrible article about yourself in the news, or learn about devastating social media error that you had made, the first thing you need to do is shake yourself out of the shock and clear your mind for the battle that may lay ahead.

3 - Know that the media and the public will be feeding on your problems

Once you have awaken up to reality, the next phase is being able to understand that what may be pain for one man, may be joy or profits for another.

And if you know how news networks and social media works, then you will understand that those outlets won't have a problem publishing anything that would maximize their readership and sales, even if the content would embarrass you, cause you harm, bring an end to your career, force your family into suicide, or even destroy your marriage.

Hence, in many cases, the media and gossip mills will always be happy to feed on any negative, controversial or reader interesting thing about you, even if the materials that they publish are not entirely true.

Therefore, you must understand that whenever a story, a rumor, a sensational video, a controversial photo, or anything interesting about you hits the news, social media or the gossip mill, there are always people and news syndicates that are always desperate and ready to amplify it, repeat it, or twist it.

So do not be surprised if a negative news item or a rumor about you finds itself on the front burner of social media discussions or the newscast for a longer period than you would have expected.

After all, and as I had said before; - the media would be feeding on your reputation degrading problems, much to the desire of their insatiable news readers and viewers.

4 - Do not panic. Remain calm

It is never a pleasant experience to turn on the television or open up the newspaper only to see your name and your photograph strapped under a dirty, humiliating or criminal-sounding headline.

For most people, an immediate state of confusion, fear, embarrassment, and sustained panic can step in.

And when someone is dragged into a sudden state of panicking, their instinctive response to such a scenario can turn out to be devastating and even life threatening, depending on a number of factors.

But while panicking may be our first psychological response to any sudden onset of fear, surprise or some other form of emotional discomfort, it can have a negative impact on your ability to think clearly and act wisely in a crisis situation as discussed early on.

And when your face and name is associated with something nasty in the news; that is one time in which there is no room for a panicking state, even though nature would naturally push you into that mode.

Hence, in such a scenario, you must ensure that you do not panic, but remain calm, no matter how severe, untrue, degrading, or amplified the media mentions about you may be.

5 - Quietly accept guilt and reject the lies where necessary

One thing that you must understand is that all a news hawker would need to make you look bad is to ensure that there is at least one percent of truth in whatever negative content that they want to publish about you. And the rest of the material would be sensationalized enough to make your story an interesting or viral read.

But in order for you to effectively deal with a bad media crisis, you first need to determine what is factual about you in the news and what is not.

And the sooner you can quietly accept guilt where it is due (to yourself only), and reject the lies or twisted truths, the sooner you can better develop a strategy or the right frame of mind to effectively think through and deal with the issue in its entirety.

6 - Ponder first on a strategy to deal with the issue

Once your conscience is clear and your mind is set towards dealing with the issue, then it may be time for you to ponder on a strategy to get past it.

However, you may want to know that this will be a very much cautious and point twisting stage, since your decision would in effect determine where the story actually goes from there.

You must also be mindful that the media do not like to be corrected, and may not be inclined to publish a reverse story from you, since it can discredit them.

Furthermore, responding directly to media reports can also sometimes make the situation worst since some initial media reports are intended to draw you out into the open and give the media a better opportunity to amplify or continue to keep your story in the public domain.

Hence, you need to first try to determine whether the story is intended to be a one off news item, a media provocation, or a broader strategy to increase your vulnerability.

And if you are finding it difficult to determine this, please feel free to send a link or a copy of the article to me at: **adonisbooks@gmail.com**, and I will try to help you out with an assessment, or a response strategy.

7 - Do not pity yourself or allow people to pity you

Whenever something bad happens to us on a scale that strenuously tests our ability to handle severe psychological pressure, we usually become angry and pitiful of ourselves.

And while anger is understandable, the emergence of pity for yourself can actually place you into a vulnerable phase which can be easily transformed into the first stage of a mental breakdown, an emotional crisis, or extreme depression which can eventually bury you under a deep mound of media madness.

On the other hand, if you are pitied by other people that are close to you, this often directs your emotions to pity yourself which will practically lead to the same thing.

Therefore it is always best to avoid feeling sorry for yourself, and focus on being more confrontational in your thoughts of the issue instead.

This will certainly strengthen your mindset and make you both psychologically and physically stronger in the long term; but more importantly, for any existing media crisis that may be before you.

8 - Do not let go of your self-esteem or go below your worth

Any negative or humiliating media coverage of yourself can often force you into a corner that can change you for the worst, in as much that you can suddenly find yourself having a low self-esteem and exhibiting a feeling of worthlessness.

And if you should allow that to happen, I can assure you that you will be heading down a sinkhole that you might never be able to recover from.

As such, it is imperative that you try to keep your mindset of your self-worth at the upper level where it has always been, since you will certainly be needing it for the remainder of your battle with negative media coverage.

9 - Apologize cautiously and selectively, but do not remain continuously apologetic

When you are portrayed nastily in the media, the people who are closest to you or who felt that they are somehow directly or indirectly affected, can become an emotional pain to your conscience.

In essence, if a man is highlighted as a wrong doer he is often forced to apologize to his wife, his children and any other person who may have suffered collateral damage as a result of his media troubles.

And of course in such cases, it is always wise to apologize to people only where an apology is genuinely due, and deserving. But you must be careful about what you are actually apologizing for.

Because if the information about you in the media is untrue, is twisted or ultimately altered, then you ought to specifically apologize to those closest to you for the embarrassment that the media outlets have caused them by exploiting your name.

After all, if you carelessly apologize for something you did not do, or for a story that was altered from the truth, then people are bound to tie you to the exact contents of the articles.

That aside, you should consider using a short period of your crisis time to apologize, if it is actually warranted. Otherwise, you should not go around apologizing continuously or extensively to everyone.

Over apologizing in any scenario often lead observers to think or assume that you are guilty, and is now repeatedly asking for redemption, or the public's forgiveness.

10 - Do not be what the media say you are

A news publication that embraces the sensationalizing of a story or any article writer with harmful motives generally has a natural tendency to effectively brand a person's character with unsavory titles, pseudonyms, phrases, and accolades that can add a desired effect on a reader's mind.

In essence, if a journalist or a news publication is desirous of causing the public to see you as a fraudster or a problematic character (for example) then the articles will be designed to cause the reader to believe that is what you are.

And sometimes to emphasize their intent, the publication or multiple publications can repeatedly refer to the same form of characterization either for the sake of being an innocent copycat, or to simply achieve a particular goal, such as humiliating you.

But if you are to successfully overcome your media struggles and outwit any media branding that might be out there, then you first have to ensure that you do not live as the character that is being portrayed by the media or allowing yourself to be aligned to it.

11 – Wait it out. Give the issue some time

Stop stressing out yourself. Because no one article or multiple articles about you will ever be published for every single day of the year.

People will become fed up of the story about you being repeating itself, and even the media themselves would become wary of the subject matter.

So, if you can accept that time heals, then you can accept my advice to simply wait it out. The drama about you in the news and social media would all be over sooner than you may think. They always do.

12 – After the Crisis: Carefully decide what life changes you want to make

A negative media onslaught can last for a few hours, several days, or even a few weeks with the same sustained interest from the public.

But regardless of how long it may have lasted, it has to come to an end, and will come to an end.

And when it does fold-up all of its interested in you, then it will be up to you clean your wounds and move forward on the proverbial battle field.

Therefore, there are certain decisions that you may have to make in the interest of yourself, your family your career, and all else that matters to you.

Among the first things to consider, is whether you can actually make any real change from where you were living when the negativities first became public.

After all, a nasty media exposure or drama can certainly degrade your standing in a community or bring great embarrassment upon yourself or your family.

But trust me on this. Moving out because you are too embarrassed to face your neighbors is not always the best thing to do.

In the same way, quitting your local job to run away to a new community does not always work out either.

And I will tell you why.

First of all running away from your community always gives the wrong impression that you are guilty and is ashamed of your guilt or is unable to prove your innocence.

Secondly, if you have been living in a community for quite some time, there are certainly a number of people there who already know you and may be very much inclined to forgive you or at least tolerate you in despite of whatever negativity they would have heard on TV or had seen in the newspaper about you.

Thirdly, in this day and age of the internet, it is not difficult for someone to look you up on a search engine, only to find the same negative content that you may be trying to run away from.

After all, people often turn to search engines, since it is an easy and accessible tool, to query or dig up information about strangers.

So imagine moving into a new neighborhood and befriending the community and gaining their trust, only to arouse their fears later after one of them would have seek out some disturbing information about you from a media post on the internet.

You better believe that in such a case, your new neighbors, employers or business associates will feel betrayed, and may be more fearful of you, in as much that they would press in all ways possible to see you leave, or will simply avoid you altogether.

And if the sanity of your family and sense of humiliation is anything that really matters, then I am sure that you would not want community isolation to be a contributing factor to it.

That being said, you will certainly have to weigh whether the scale of your media drama would mean a smaller, greater or no life changes at all, and if so, what they should be.

Because some changes can make things worse, while others can certainly be for the good of yourself, your family, and your collective future.

But if you need someone to discuss this with or simply need a second opinion, then I will be happy to reach out to you, if you can connect with me via email: **adonisbooks@gmail.com**.

13 – Do not stick in your past, move on.

When there are bad things about you in the media, you would naturally find it difficult to get past the nightmares especially if the negativities are impeding your overall progress or is serving as a stumbling block for every effort that you have been making.

And because we are in the age of the internet, past negative media publications about your person is practically a repeating pain because it is always there and is always syndicated by Google or other major search engines,

Hence it does not actually go away from the realm of reality. But remains in virtual circulation practically for digital eternity.

Therefore, you will only be hurting yourself and those around you if you decide to stick your life around those media negativities.

But if you are serious about redefining your future and about strengthening your overall prospects, then you will know that no matter how painstaking it can be, you must leave the media negativities of your past behind you, and simply move on.

14 - Do not forsake old relationships but build new ones

Whenever you have a life changing experience such as a sustained negative media mincing, then I can tell you that even some of your friends or acquaintances would either abruptly or gradually crawl away from you. After all, loyalty is a difficult asset to acquire these days.

Don't be surprised to see the very people that you embrace turn out to be the same ones that have been using online pseudonyms to make negative comments under a humiliating article about you.

Do not be surprised to know that some of your closest allies are the ones that will actually "like" and ensure that they further share a negative article that is online about you.

Do not be surprised if they are smiling with you but are actually smiling sarcastically at you.

Unfortunately, that is one of life's many bad lessons. And whether you like it or not it is one class that you will have to take.

But looking at things in a broader context, you often do not know who are the people that are really by your side or who are the people that would stick with you through thick and thin; until an event such as a disgraceful media episode about you, comes their way.

I can tell you that in such a case, many of them would unhesitatingly tie their shoe laces and run from your side.

And in such a case, the passage of life requires that you simply replace those disloyal friends, with new ones.

Hence, as bad as things may sound about you out there, you will and you must build new relationships to regain your mental strength and willingness to take life challenges by the horn.

But at the same time, while you are building new relationships, you will still need many of the old ones.

Therefore, do not forsake all of them during your life changing processes; - because, some of them would be more than worthy for you to keep.

15 - Experiment with dignified career changes if necessary

Some media negativity can have a lasting impact on certain classes of careers in as much that it can become difficult for you to actually land a real job in that field ever again.

For example, if you are a bank supervisor who the media has branded as a client fraudster or an alleged cash pilfering agent, then rest assure that another bank or the financial services sector or another major company will not be so eager to employ you.

Even if you are exonerated at a trial or no wrong was actually found on your part, the negativity that was there in the first instance would actually serve as the potential nail in your career's coffin.

And in such a case, a complete career change may become a necessity.

This can range from providing non-intrusive financial consultancy services (if you are into finances), to opting into a non-qualification required field such as operating a diner, an auto rental company, a freighting company or something that can match your prior earnings or long term financial goals.

As a matter of fact, and from a serious point of view, there are more than a thousand other career changes that you can make without having to re-invest too much into your education or even yourself.

But if you cannot decide or you need some advice on what may be best for your circumstances, I will be more than happy to share my opinion if you can connect with me at: **adonisbooks@gmail.com**.

16 - Accept that there are negative things that are out there on you

One of the most failed things that you can do after a round of media humiliation is to bury your head in the sand as if the negative sayings about you will remain buried there too.

After all, and no matter how you may want to twist it, the same negative story will still be stuck in the internet archives and on most people's minds practically forever.

And the sooner you can accept that those negative sayings about you will always be there, the more prepared and stronger you will be to manage and overcome the challenges that may waiting ahead.

17 - Acknowledge your awareness of those negativities in your dealings

While you may be on a new career quest or may be busy building new relationships, you will certainly have to deal with the pain of fair and safe disclosures as it relates to your negative media mentions, or your media checkered past.

By all accounts, most people prefer to have a better understanding of who they are dealing with, in addition to who the media is insinuating you to be.

After all, they would indirectly prefer to make their own assessment of who you really are.

Therefore, it might be best to keep an addendum that you can label as (for example)"character disclosures, criminal disclosures, or concerned information", which you can attach at the end of business proposals, job applications or other communication that would require the other person's review for consideration.

Trust me on this; people and companies appreciate it when you can be honest and straight forward with them about your past media accusations or indiscretions from the inception; and would immediately have an interest in working with you or hiring you even conditionally.

Because in any case, due diligence might pick up these negative media reports in the long term, which can certainly result in you being distrusted and losing out on new employment opportunities and new business relationships.

However, disclosures must always be constructive and can be offered as an addendum to your job application, a visa application, a business proposal, or any other documentation that will actually go up for sensitive consideration.

18 - Know that your bad media reputation might precede you

Whenever the media gives you a bad reputation, you can rest assure that it will precede you on many fronts, though not necessarily all.

But rest assure that even in cases where due diligence is not required, basic media information about you can be a determining factor in your social or simple business interfacing with people.

That being the case, you must always be cognizant of how you can be viewed.

In other words, you will have to be cautious in your engagement with people who might want to use your media reputation as a bargaining tool, or as an element to force you into compromising in situations that you would not normally entertain.

However, being aware that a bad media reputa-

-tion may precede you, can certainly give you some needed advantages.

For sure, it will certainly keep you in a prepared state of mind, and can also help you to better manage your interactions with the public, as a whole.

19 -Always confront that bad media reputation constructively

When you carry a bad media reputation, your reputation itself in the eyes of the unthinking public may equally be considered as bad.

And that may be all someone or a rival may need to repeatedly humiliate, blackmail, undermine, or deter you.

Therefore, do not be surprise if someone who wishes to entertain a crowd or humiliate you, might find it useful to sarcastically raise your negative media mentions to you in a public place or in a scenario where you may more than likely be left in an embarrassing position.

While your provoker might be expecting a confrontational response to trigger more humiliation, it is better to simply nod your head in disgust and walk away from the perpetrator or simply question his/her ability to decipher what they actually read, before walking away.

Constructive confrontation is also always useful in one-on-one debates about any media mentions where you felt it necessary to make your point.

Otherwise, avoiding gathering in public places just after your media debacle or simply walking away from one would always remain the best option.

20 – Be truthful about your past, and you will have no need to be afraid of the future

As I had mentioned earlier, disclosures will become an important factor in your dealings, after suffering a nasty media onslaught, and characterization of your person.

People would be more apprehensive and distrusting if they were the one who had to unravel your dirty media mentions.

Worst off, it will be more painful if someone else or some other entity had to disclose this to them.

But if you are the one who has disclosed it, then they will most likely be inclined to trust you and possibly prefer your side of the story.

Moreover, you won't have to live with the fear of looking over your shoulder, or having to be worried about what would happen if the negative things that were said about you in the media, comes to light at some point in the future.

Therefore, as long as you have to engage in business activities, relationship building, or have to be delegated to a trusted position, it will be in your best interest to always be honest enough to let the other person or entity be aware of your past media-fueled negativities.

And even though you might lose three out of ten opportunities by doing that, the other seven would certainly worth your honest decision to be truthful to people about your past.

21 - Still seek out opportunities. The doors are never really closed

Most people who have experienced negative media exposures tends to become reclusive and career shy, and can find it difficult to move their lives forward in a positive way.

And this is usually as a result of them developing a low self-esteem, and a loss of self-confidence, compounded by an embedded sense of media fear, prolonged anger, hurt, distrust and a revolving form of humiliation.

As a result, they are usually afraid of seeking out new opportunities or expanding their own career goals.

But believe me, there may be someone, some

company, or some entity somewhere that actually needs your skill, and may be willing to overlook your purported transgressions or negative media reports, just to retain you.

However, you would not know this, neither would the people who hold the key to the rebirth of your career, unless you actually make an effort to seek out new opportunities.

22 – Show people who you really are

While the media would go at lengths to characterize you, often in the most demeaning and negative ways, as I had told you earlier, you do not have to be the character that they portray you to be.

The media telling the public that you are client pilfering accountant or an abusive man may not realistically be the person that you are. But research has shown that people who have been repeatedly characterized by the media can become psychologically entrapped and forced to adapt and accept the character that was assigned to them.

And from the moment you are forced to believe that you are of a certain character and you accept that classification, then in time to come you can evolve into the person that you are portrayed to be.

Therefore, I will want to caution you that negative media mentions have other forms of effects on you and can create an almost irreparable identity crisis.

That being the case, you must maintain your character's status quo, and be real about who you are.

And if you can demonstrate your true self throughout your media debacles then there are people who would actually be appreciative of your reputation challenges, and the real side of you.

23 - Remember that the fight for redemption is never over

You might be the guy who was in the news in the most degrading and negative way five years ago, but the Good Samaritan who have been helping dozens of children to go back to school or the one who has been saving them from starvation for over four years.

But if you ask me, I can safely tell you that detractors would always find a way to get to you if they want to, and which will in essence drown out the good side of your life.

Therefore, do not be surprised if you help an old lady to cross the street, and the media say that in one line, while dedicating a thousand other lines to embarrassing elements of your past.

And though you might be more discouraged, I can assure you that it can't get any worst.

So don't let a negative repeat of your story in the media from a decade ago distract you.

Because, just as it had all come to an end the first time, so will it come to an end again. And then possibly repeat itself again, and again.

After all, the fight for redemption is never a done battle. So regrettably you might have to go through the same processes that are highlighted in this book, all over again.

24 - Pursue your goals and your dreams, because they may still be waiting for you

As discussed earlier, negative media mentions can have a lifelong impact on a person's career goals, their business relationships, and marriage among other things.

But most of all, it creates a veil of fear that often forces an individual to give up their lifelong dreams and aspirations.

However, repeated research has shown that people with negative media mentions were still able to achieve their life goals, which in turn has helped them to renew their life and gain new desired opportunities.

After all, a remarkable achievement is often deemed as a form of reformation.

So if you really want to escape the clutches of media negativity, go right ahead and pursue your life dreams. Because you might be surprised to know that it is still out there waiting for you.

25 - You are not a major part of the world's problems. People will forgive and forget anyway

Sometimes, it is good to be a little bold and stick your middle finger out at the people who had made efforts via the media to ruin you, humiliate you and embarrass you.

Because in reality, you are not a major part of the world's problems.

Our planet and its residents are too depressed with their own troubles. And whether you want to believe it or not, the very readers who would have chastised and ridiculed you, will forgive and forget about you some day. They always do.

● Where to get help

During a negative media crisis, you have to always be mindful of where you go for help. Because, some of the same people that might be calling to comfort you, might be the same ones who are actually hounding around for more information from you.

That aside, the news media often targets the people that are closely linked to you for information. And in many cases, additional information can either be deliberately handed over to a journalist or be inadvertently dispensed out of anger or provocation from a teasing journalist.

Therefore, it is usually better to first alert your family lawyer of what is happening, and turn to a media professional or a reliable support person for help.

That aside, I am always willing and inclined to offer my advice and guidance to person's whose reputation is under threat from the media, or who may be looking to find a way to redeem themselves.

So if you want to throw some of your concerns my way, please feel free to send me a message by email to: **adonisbooks@gmail.com**.

● How to put together a crisis speech

Not every time a media crisis or a negative media report on you will require a public response.

As a matter of fact, you have to remain mindful about public responses, since some can actually work for you, or can work against you if the media is bent on twisting your story to achieve a particular goal.

But even when there are no public statements or media responses, it may be wise to at least give a mild explanation or support speech to the people within your company, or any other organization that you may be a member of; and whose support you may very well need to survive a negative media onslaught.

While there are a number of things that you can say, or a number of ways in which you can say it, an internal crisis speech must have certain elements in order for it to actually work.

First, you must appear and sound confident but a little broken while making your speech. After all, people resonate better with your emotions and must be able to see that you are actually struggling to find your strength during the crisis.

Within the speech itself, there must also be a particular approach, tone and flow.

That is to mean that you approach your listeners by thanking them for giving you an hearing, and then letting them know that you have been hit by some negative media coverage (which most of them would have already know anyhow).

While you can give an indication of what the negativity may be, it might be better to be a little vague and make reference to elements of the headlined story or the bottom line, only.

Because, if you dig too deep into the issue at hand, you might certainly be opening up yourself to more questions than answers.

But once you have made them aware of the negativity at hand, you can move on to say how it has impacted you and your family, and your worry about how it can impact the people who work close to you.

Nonetheless, you must swiftly deny the reports or elements of the news reports (whichever may be appropriate, and bring in your listeners by pleading with them to vouch for you, in the same way that you would have vouched for them because they know your character, in the same way that you know theirs.

At the same time, do not pressure them to believe you or urge them to believe you. Instead it will be most wise to ask them not to be hasty in their judgment and to allow you an opportunity to address the negativity and unveil the truth.

And during your crisis you just need them to be patient as you work to address the matter, in addition to subsequently proving your innocence.

In the end, try to make the speech short but non-rushing, while letting your colleagues know that you are open to individually discuss the issue with each of them in the comfort of your office space whenever it is mutually convenient.

Thereafter, you are bound to have some support from your colleagues which you may need throughout your negative media crisis.

However, you must be mindful and be careful not to drag any of your supporters into your media troubles, such as causing them to go to the press to represent you or sending out a statement for you.

This type of intervention can sometimes backfire on you, and can often lead to an extension of the crisis.

● Example crisis speech

If you are not certain about how your crisis speech to your colleagues should flow, I have enclosed a simple and straightforward example here, which I am sure you may find useful, with a little bit of modification to suit your individual situation.

"Good morning to you all, and thank you for being here with me at this very dark moment.

Today has been one of the most difficult days for me, my family, and for the people like you who had always looked up to me, and always had great thoughts of me.

I am saying this is one of my most difficult days because of a very damaging report that has been circulating about me in the press and social media.

For those who do not know or have heard about this devastating report, I will point it to you shortly, but wish to let you know that the news report in question is centered on an allegation that "(for example) during my tenure at Monroe and Company, I had sexually assaulted two employees"

I can immediately say to you that the report and the accusations itself is filled with twisting lines and lies, intended only to degrade me to a state of shame and distrust, and to further ruin my reputation and my career.

For those of you who do not know me, I can assure you that I am not that type of man that is being described in that news report. And to those who really know me, you will know that I am not that type of person, and will never be that type of person.

You will know that I am a person who respects and value my peers, and those under my supervision in as much that I see myself as their workplace guardian and counselor.

Hence, if nothing else you will equally agree that the news reports that are currently circulating about me is a concoction of lies, and certainly intended to paint me as a monster.

While I am currently reviewing my legal options regarding these many damaging untruths that have been published about me, I will sincerely ask for your support and patience at this difficult time, and to not rush to any judgment against me.

I know this may be hard, but it is something that I am certain that I would have done for anyone of you here if you were in the same position, because I know that I also work with good people who would not do such a dirty thing either.

Moreover, I am not asking you to defend me or to preach the gospel for me. All I am simply asking, is for you to please stand by myself and my family's side through this difficult moment, since only your support can help me, my devastated wife, and my kids, to evade emotional insanity.

Thanking you in anticipation for being there for me, and for lending me your support.

Whoever wishes to receive a link to the article, and wish to offer me any advice or ask any question I am currently open to you at my desk. So you can come over and let's have a chat.

Thanks again".

NOTE: if you are looking for help with a crisis speech, please feel free to reach out to me at: **adonisbooks@gmail.com**, and I will try to help you in the best way I can.

● My conclusion

It is often amazing how mankind's generic way of thinking and a basic piece of news media information (whether factual or false) can actually become the *de facto* arbiter of a person's reputation, or can actually influence public opinion on whether you are a good person or not.

Furthermore, it is quite sad to note how simple and how easy it is to lose your reputation, and your needed trust among men.

Moreover, it is even more painful, when one has to consider the fact that a person may have to live with a media-tainted character all of their lives, and for which there might never be any real redemption for a good reputation that is now lost.

But in reality, losing your good reputation does not necessarily denote that you should lose your dreams too, or lose your friends, your family, your future, your aspirations, or anything that matters to you, unless you choose to let them go.

However, at the same time, it will be difficult to pull many people's shoulder closer to your side during your media troubled times, while having the actual zeal to survive the psychological suffering that reputation degradation brings.

In reality, persevering above it all can naturally become an elusive quest.

It is for that very reason that I had found it necessary to write this book, so that it can serve as a self-supporting manual during your media troubles, especially when no one actually wants to be close to you or close to the embarrassment that negative news reporting can bring.

Now, while I was able to effectively put together this book based upon the researches of a respected behavioral psychologist, several contributing news editors, and the proven experiences of more than a dozen reputation degradation victims (including myself); - I can only hope that the mythology that I have given you in this book would be of great help to you, in your quest for redemption of your good name.

But in despite of my optimism and my advises as a whole, I want you to understand that the true battle to regain the reputation that you may have lost through the negative portrayal of your character in the media is usually just yours to fight.

Because no matter how many advices that you may have, and how many consoling there may be; your path to recovery can only be possible if you can actually put those advices and your willingness to the wheel of time, and be patient with redemption as it is patient with you.

After all, one of the things that you can be sure about is that none of us are perfect in ourselves or even in spirit.

And whenever your perceived imperfections are dragged into the light in a negative way, people will always want to feed on it; because it can supposedly bring them some form of psychological comfort about themselves as they struggle with their own dark secrets and their hidden flaws.

In reality, many people will only characterize and say bad things about you, because it is the only way in which their own insignificant self can feel better than you.

And if their imperfections or hidden secrets should come to light alongside yours, you might be surprised at the level at which you may have to drag them down on the same reputation scale that they had use to degrade you.

Sometimes, if you are fortunate to get behind the lives of the people who had penned bad things about you or who would have made bad comments about you in a news post, you might be shocked and saddened at what their true reputation would reveal.

That being said, you often do not have to feel bad about yourself, or worthless when the news media downgrades your reputation.

Because a negative news report about you does not necessarily reflect the real you, and should not be the one element to control your life, your dreams and aspirations, or your destiny.

Actually, a concentrated group of people's perception of your reputation would never be the belief or the opinion of the entire planet.

So while it may be great for you to follow twenty five, thirty five or fifty five guidelines about rebuilding your life and your reputation from a book, rest assure that you do not really need to perfect or emulate any of it.

Because in reality, you do not necessarily need to sit on someone else's opinion to actually chart your own paths, conquer your mistakes and rebuild your reputation.

So, whenever the media attacks your reputation and public opinion grades you down, the will-power to take a stand, battle through it all, and be yourself again, is actually yours!

So in my final words to you, I want to let you know that it is quite ok for you to gently stick your middle finger out to your reputation degraders, and tell them to bring it on, because you are rising up from the canvas again.

After all, no one really knows you better than yourself.

♦ *Dennis E. Adonis*